Making Lemonade

A Positive Outlook During Times of Adversity

Steve Fryman

Making Lemonade

A Positive Outlook During Times of Adversity

C   2020 by Steve Fryman

ISBN: 978-0-578-69852-6

Printed in the united states of America.

About the Author

Steve Fryman is a lifelong learner who has dedicated his life to overcoming adversity thru the art of making lemonade one pitcher at a time He hopes this book is helpful in your search for answers to nagging problems we all face while making lemonade

E-mails:

sfryman2004gmail.com
steve@makinglemonadethebookclub.com

Website:

https//makinglemonadethebookclub.com

Dedication

To my best friend and Wife who I have learned so much from;
helping me to love again.

Note from the Author

This book has been extremely difficult to write from an emotional and technical standpoint. I respect the time you are willing to invest in reading this book and apologize for my short comings as a communicator. I realize you can not be in my head. I do hope that being honest and vulnerable sharing my heart will make up for my lack of writing abilities. My hope for you as the reader will look at this book as an opportunity to relate to your challenges, exploring solutions to your issues.

Making Lemonade is not an elegant piece of literature. It is far from anything that even resembles a coherent body of work. My intentions are to be helpful; letting you know you are not alone in your challenges. Offering options and possibilities you may not have considered. The timeline through the book can often be confusing, my apologies. Look at each topic and section as part of a puzzle. Hopefully, this jigsaw puzzle will make sense once the corners are put in place for orientation. When put together the puzzle should look like the picture on the cover. I am thankful for gifted Editors who can help readers hear the voice of the writer more clearly.

I know you have a story to tell. There is a workbook that was created to help you tell your story. The workbook will be published shortly after this book is released. There is Something about taking the time to ponder and write answers to pointed questions. I believe this is a positive step to resolving some difficult issues that hold us back and stunt our growth as people.

Making Lemonade

A Positive Outlook During Times of Adversity

Introduction:

An old saying "When Life gives you lemons Make Lemonade"

What are the ingredients for the recipe needed to turn despair into victory?

We understand things worth doing are easy to say and hard to carry out without help......

In these times of difficulty, it feels as though finding the elusive right attitude is unattainable. This frustration leads us down the road of self-pity causing us to self-medicate, setting foot on a destructive and demoralizing path. We can feel as though we are spiraling downwards out of control.

Our negative behavior corrodes and numb, scaring our hearts. We look for temporary respite from the hurt. This pain is meant for our growth. It is good to suffer for doing good. We need to learn from tests and trials. If learning takes place, we will not repeat the things that caused us difficulty. As lifelong learners we will prevail over adversity. Otherwise we are relearning the same lessons our entire life.

Permanent positive changes lessen the effects of reoccurring negative cycles that get passed on from generation to generation.

Sadly, if not put into check our pain becomes compounded making us feel helpless with thoughts that things will never change. This unfortunately often complicates matters. Making the core issues worse, and harder to attain a solution. With proper perspective the solutions are within our reach, no need to prolonging needless suffering. For those issues that need more time to resolve. We can make small incremental changes; the sum will add up to a notable defined change with resolution. How do we continue to keep moving forward. {We will explore more in depth later} What does it take to turn the smoldering fire of despair into the blazing flames of encouragement which can heal and revitalize our battle torn hearts? At times we may need to dig deep as we learn to make lemonade out of difficult situation. As we experience victory; success builds on success making issues more manageable. Please understand that there's lots of ingredient that go into making Lemonade. ***We will learn more about the 2 primary ingredients that can neutralize the bitter acid in the lemons making lemonade drinkable. Water and Sweetener***

In these pages we will explore what it takes to make world class Lemonade. It's not enough to just survive a deluge of lemons. We can learn to thrive when faced with what seems like an untenable set of circumstances, trials and challenges. Learning perseverance is a grinding proses that no one likes, however the valuable resolve attained by the lessons makes it worthwhile. Growing from lessons learned from hardship.

Lemonade production can often be difficult due to our general outlook. Our negative personality traits can hinder us learning valuable lessons. If you're like me, you like to have a certain amount of control over your surroundings, invariably there are usually strong variables which come in the form of challenges/trials that are completely out of our control. We must make a concise effort to deal with lemons quickly. If not dealt with expediently the seeds of regret will root in our hearts, giving us heart ache. This rooting will leave us feeling puckered and tuckered; emotionally exhausted. This can lead us to feelings of depression and desperation. It is terrible to feel the impending doom of Damocles sward hanging over your head every waking minute.

We have a choice as to how we respond to challenges/lemons in our life's. It is how we respond that will determine outcome. Making lemonade does not come naturally to me it has been a lifelong learning prosses. Please understand I have daily battles like everyone else. I am very much flawed, a work in progress.

Table of Contents

The History of Lemons

Why Me?

Lemons that grow on trees have been around since the beginning of time itself. The original non hybrid is called a citron and has interesting roots in Judaism with the harvest festival of Sukkot the festival of the tabernacles. The citrus is one of 4 elements essential for the celebration of tabernacles. This festival is in preparation for winter. Interesting that the lemon would be the fruit of choice by the Jews for celebrations. What can we learn from a fall celebration? Winter can be difficult and is symbolic of hard change and hardship. The citron has played a major role in the prayer life of the Jewish festival. The figurative lemons have been a centerpiece of humanities day to day lives in the form of challenges, change and trials since ancient times. In this book the term lemon will be used figuratively meaning challenges, trials and changes that occur while we are living on this planet earth. It seems every season of life has its challenges. While we live on this blue marble, we are guaranteed to have lemons in our lives. Most often our lemons have roots in discontentment and regret. If I only... you fill in the blank or I should of... could of ...and if things would have turned out differently. Sorry, you do not have a time machine; time travel is out of the question when it comes to changing the past. We know self-pity is not the answer. As you have heard before no one wants to come to our Pity Party. Please join me in the exploration of making Lemonade; that refreshing drink that quenches the need for a pity party. I have some great suggestions for sweeteners that will help un pucker the past. There is no sense in living in the past, with its bitter roots.

Charles Kettering the inventor said. *"You can't have a better tomorrow if you're* thinking *about yesterday"*

*We can learn from the past, so we do not find ourselves in an incredible spinning vortex spiraling downward. **Let's make some lemonade**!*

The Ingredients Needed to Make Lemonade - The Right Stuff

Lemons - Challenges, Problems, Change

- Getting a new boss

- Changing your Position Description -new responsibilities

- Downsizing your department[ouch]

- Hostile/toxic work environment

- Soured relationships

- Health issues

Water - Soothing, life sustaining, energy giving

- Diet

- Exercise

- Necessary for life

- Thirst Quenching

- Cleansing

- Sleep - Rest

- Room to Breath

Sweeteners - Life enhancing and more

- Faith based belief in something greater

- Having a life Coach or Mentor

- Read books that will encourage you

- Have hope that this too will pass

- Throw out the negative tapes that keep playing in your mind

- The attitude of gratitude

- Giving, serving other

- Forgive and forget

Variations of the recipe - Attitude Is Everything

- In the workplace

- At home

- When you are out and about

- While traveling

- When sending time with family

- When things are gritty

Dealing with Past - Leaving the past in the past

- Seeds-Stopping seeds from taking root

- Peels-Useful protection shielding the past

- Pulp-Some people like pulp

The Ingredients Needed to Make Lemonade

The Right Stuff

The Lemons

Lemons - Challenges, Problems, trials

Summary: Lemons = Challenges

With out lemons there would be no need to make Lemonade. I cannot imagine what life would be like without challenges. In this section we can explore a variety of challenges. This will enable you to relate better to your challenges. Empowering you to search for resolution and closure. I apologize if I sound like a victim at times; that was not intentional. Some of the problems we bring on ourselves, others are out of our control. It is how we respond to our problems that makes the difference. Will the weight of trials crush you or make you stronger? If it makes us stronger, you will be more compassionate improving your emotional intelligence. As we remain positive, we have deeper empathy seeing the commonality of difficulties, we all experience. Whether your troubles are few or many the right attitude will pay large dividends inspiring people around you Let's juice some lemons.

- The new Boss

- The ever-changing Position Description- new responsibilities

- Downsizing your department [ouch]

- Hostile/toxic work environment

- Soured Relationships

- Health issues

○ ○

Lemons   The New Boss

This is not necessarily a bad thing; well unless it is, sorry.

I have had good Bosses and bad Bosses. THE GOOD BOSS believed in you, gives you some autonomy and invested in you. You were validated, acknowledged for bringing worth to the organization. These things put a skip in your step, making Sunday nights enjoyable with no dread of Monday.

The dark force…...Bad Boss

Dreading Monday, I have been there more than a few times. You Ask yourself how I will make it thru another week. The micro-managed wheels spinning in the mud feeling. You experience your hands tied behind your back trying to second guess the response from the bad Boss who seems like he owns the **Lemon** grove.

Lemons   The ever-changing Position Description new responsibilities

Definition of **rules**:

Plural noun

1. *one of a set of explicit or understood regulations or principles governing conduct within an activity or sphere.*

2. *control of or dominion over an area or people.*

VERB

1. exercise ultimate power or authority over (an area and its people).

2. pronounce authoritatively and legally to be the case.

"You are hired!"

Magic words to your indebted ears. All the excitement of starting fresh, a new start. Oh, the places you will go and the people you will meet.

Wait just a minute …. back to reality everyone is doing more with less. At times I have felt like someone has changed the rules after we started the game. For you American Football fans it is like extending the goal posts another 30 yards after the game started. Sorry another sport analogy.

The National Anthem plays, the first pitch is thrown out and the fences are extended out on the playing field *200 more feet*. Everything in you s c r e a m s FOWL…………… *Ok, Time Out* whistle blows, officials please reset the game clock.

Smells like **Lemons** to me

Let's get a grip here. Please remain calm consider these options.

- Time to take stock of the situation at hand, reality check do not make any life changing decisions while you are upset

- The attitude of gratitude is a sweetener; ask yourself if you are being ungrateful *{talk more about this later- see Sweeteners}*

- Thinking about looking for another job? We know the grass is not always greener- perhaps you can trust the evil you know

- Are things so difficult that you cannot grow thru the situation

* Are you always discontented causing you to be a job hopper?

* There is a time that it is good to move on, is this the time?

* If you are going to leave, find a job before you leave the current one it is easier to get a job when you already have a job.

Lemons   Downsizing your department *[ouch]*

This is a tough one. An oversized big rig jammed full of **Lemons**!

Three and a half years ago I got a new boss-had my position description changed *[do you see the progression] and was downsized. This is one of the most painful* experiences of my professional life. Yes, I admit we were somewhat overstaffed.

I think the hardest thing was the way the downsizing took place. There was a series of meetings where my subdominants were encouraged to play beat on the Supervisor by the change manager.

I am not wanting to sound like a victim. All emotion and feelings aside. I would like to share the facts and try to recreate what took place in the downsizing process. Adjustments in my team would have had to come from the Inside out; with the employees requesting the changes

I work for a state entity where it is near imposable to terminate employees. There are only a few instances where termination will occur:

Fighting on the job	Stealing and scavenging
Bringing a gun to work	Job Abandonment

I found myself in the middle of a hostile work environment I sought help from Human Resources and got none…. Human Resources is neither human nor resourceful.

I was very close to hiring an Attorney. Spoke to an attorney who specializes in hostile work environment. The Attorney said to start a lawsuit I needed vast amounts of documentation which I did not have.

A few months went by and we were not having as many meetings. A lot of the position changes had taken place by way of employees transferring to different departments. The change manager had achieved his goal.

At this time there was a lot of passive aggressive behavior that was coming from the Employees that remained on my team. Until one day a line was crossed, involving damaging of state property. I called the police and made a police report. After I made a police report all the trouble stopped, a faucet had been turned off. I never knew who was doing all the demeaning aggravating things. I was the first one to arrive in the morning opening the work area. You never knew what you would find. Things would purposely be put on the floor or moved out of place. You could walk into a coat rack that was put in the doorway blocking the entrance to a room. Items were moved or missing all over the office. The team of 7 turned into 4 employee and then 2 were left. Eventually one of the two retired leaving 1 employee and me. Fortunately, the one that was left was very hard working and had a great skill set. Oddly enough I would later figure out that it was this person that was responsible for most of the passive aggressive behavior. I still struggle with forgiveness with this person because there is a strong feeling of betrayal; we will talk more about forgiveness. If you have ever experienced the combination of a hostile toxic work environment and downsizing, you become grateful for not experiencing the hostility. You gratefully accept the fact you are taking on the responsibilities of 3 employees. The extra responsibilities do not bother you as much because you have a sense of peace in your work environment. Not sure if it was planned that way or it just was a byproduct of all the change.

Remember all these changes took place over two and a half years. The first year of the two and a half years was by far the worst. There were many hours of counseling. This meant weekly trips to the Employee Assistance Program counselor. EAP is a wonderful benefit, sad to say more people should take advantage of it. Instead, people choose to suffer in silence not processing the lemons in life. I had a wonderful counselor who understood the difficult issues I was dealing with. That made a big difference to me; it was nice to have someone that was objective. People that care about you get sick of listening to you, venting the same issues all the time. At times I got tired of listening to myself.

If you have experienced times of plenty, short staffing is challenging. You certainly learn how to work more efficiently.

"Doing more with less"

The mantra in the new millennium.

This is a hard lemon to squeeze because *you feel* the squeeze to perform and complete additional tasks.

You can cut staffing but cutting to the bone is painful. Customers have been very understanding and patient. Generally, if I explain my circumstances to Joe or Jan customer WHY they must wait for services they understand. This sets expectations and helps the clock ticking in their head to be set to real time as opposed to how things were in the past when there was an abundance of help. I know I am not the only one in this kind of situation. It seems that everyone I speak to is experiencing a similar thing. Don't you wish you could clone yourself? Not sure if anyone wants more than one of me. It would be helpful though.

I have found the best way to squeeze this hard lemon is to keep things in perspective. The first thing you will want to do is get resentful, resist. Especially if you see another department adding employees. Pace yourself for a marathon not knowing if there will be relief. I went a year and a half before I could get additional help. I was shorted 2 employees that worked a walk-up window providing services. The window has a bell to ring for service. I would need to run from a back office to the service window when the bell is rung. This was especially difficult if I was on a phone call. If you find yourself in a situation like this, resist wanting to hurt the folks that ring the bell multiple times. Take the high road and think what it would be like to be in their shoes.

I felt like a human jack in the box. I always try to smile; I think it sends a message to my brain that says I am happy. *Try it sometime!* There is probably a TED talk about it. LOL...... I was offered additional help. A part time employee working 28 hours a week. I am so grateful to have this help. It has taken the edge off, especially during peak times which are seasonal.

Another part of an area I oversee was cut in half from 4 to 2 service technicians this also has taken some getting used to. The relief offered in this situation is supplementing excess work in the field to private contractors. Downsizing does not take into consideration people retiring, workers leaving, getting sick, or problems with absenteeism; the classic Friday, Monday calling out sick.

[**F**amily **M**edical **L**eave **A**ct]

A person that qualifies for FMLA can call out sick and is not required to give a reason for their absence. FMLA is a good thing and is meant to protect workers jobs. When misused or abused by employees gaming the system; it can be difficult to manage These gamers on FMLA would work harder trying to get out of work than doing the work.

With so much pressure to perform, we need to work smarter. Figure out what that looks like to you; then act on it. At some point we need to examine what are our core spiritual beliefs.

Where is the well you draw your inspiration from? What gives you strength and encouragement? Do you believe in a greater force than yourself?

Let's continue to think about this as we read thru the book

Lemons   Hostile work environment

The group I supervised was multigenerational with strong personalities; a challenging group to supervise under normal conditions.

The change manager knew how to ignite and magnify the dissatisfaction of the group. He created an even more toxic environment instituting an open-door policy. This was the beginning of the end. The policy's purpose was meant to cannibalize the Supervisor by the Staff by creating dissension in the ranks. Very effective. Special one on one meetings were created to listen to staff complaints about their Supervisor with and without the Supervisor present. Unfortunately, the change manager was a present third party but did not mediate the meetings.

All discussion was one sided coming from the Staff member with the Supervisor taking the beating. This was very hurtful, becoming a human punching bag. This was done so the workers could leave the department or asked to be reassigned.

With all honesty it was hard to see the end game when all the meetings were taking place.

Rugby players are not the only teams that eat their dead.

One of the things that ensued from the special non mediated one on one's were allegations of racism. This was an especially bitter lemon and could not be further from the truth.

In addition:

My subordinates posted my annual salary in public areas in the workplace. Demining caricatures put in restrooms and bulletin boards. Stuff you would imagine experiencing in middle school. *I will talk more about overcoming the toxic work environment later in this book.*

This was difficult because the advice I received from my Boss and Human Resources was that I should ignore it and it will stop. I did as they suggested, and it became worse.

Lemons   Soured Relationships

In this section I would like to explore how good can come out of a soured relationship.

We do not need statistics to tell us that divorce is prevalent in our culture.

I would like to share with you what I learned from a broken marriage of 10 years.

What was learned after the breakup?

- Friendship First is the most important thing in a marriage, what was the foundation of my marriage built on?

- Materialism, things are not as important as we think

- A fresh start is healthy

- The hurt is lessoned over the years; time heals

- It would have been more difficult if there were children involved

- It may have not been the best thing for me to get married at the age of 21

- Forgiveness is hard when you have been betrayed

- You will be able to trust/love again

- God loves you and wants to heal you

- Second chances are special

How can something so hurtful and destructive be learned from?

8 years into a 10-year marriage I discovered my wife did not want to be married. The beginning of the end started with a Surprise Lemon.

The Surprise **Lemon**

There was a deceptive story about a trip to visit with a friend; something did not feel right about the story.

Shortly after hearing the story about the upcoming trip I made an earth-shaking discovery. I discovered plane tickets hidden in a bag of donation items reveling the truth about the trip.

I remember coming across the tickets by accident. Thinking why I would have kept old plane tickets. Looking closer the dates matched the upcoming trip; my wife had planned to see a friend.

After discussing my discovery of the plane tickets with a mutual friend; one of my wife's confidants. I was told about someone at her work that she had developed a relationship with. The classic office romance and affair.

I saw stunned, I knew things were not great, but I did not see this coming. Naturally the timing could not have been worse. I was starting a new business and was in debt to my eyeballs. After discussion about the affair with my wife. She moved out to an undisclosed location. This separation went on for 2 years. The Attorney's fees were stacking up at the tune of $250.00 per hour, modest by todays rates. I was commuting to another city daily where I was establishing the new business.

I remember being in tremendous emotional upheaval and begging GOD to help me. As I was working in the new city, I was meeting a lot of people. On four separate occasions whether in person or on the phone I was invited to a church. Did not realize these 4 different people were from the same church.

I was not a church goer and placed little or no value as to how going to church was going to be helpful. Now you do remember me saying I was begging GOD for help. He was trying to help but I was not listening or aware of his rescue plans.

I remember this day well as if it were yesterday. It was a Wednesday around 6:30pm as the sun was setting, I pulled up in front of a church building on my way to the interstate for the commute home. I saw someone going into the building. I asked them if they would study the bible with me? Also asked did they know of anyone I could rent a room from because I need to rent out the townhome, I was living in. The man {let's call him Bobby} took my phone number and said he would let me know.

I did not think I would hear from him. A few weeks went by. Enough time for household items his and hers to be split up and put into storage. Could never imagine myself in this situation. With one suitcase I rented a hotel room and moved cities. Did not know anyone in that city. It was not too long, Bobby from the church called me. I was surprised I did not expect to hear from him Meanwhile the lord was working all the details for the rescue. Bobby came to visit me a few times and we even went for a run together. We became friends and he asked me to go to a party that a friend was hosting. My social calendar was not exactly full, so I went. It was a modest home on the water. This party was for a young Woman who was moving to Argentina to be a Missionary. The thing that impressed me was the love they had for one another. It was so amazing to hear and see amazing love like that. The woman {let's call her J} had worked for the church and was having songs sang to her and many well wishes for a safe trip to Argentina. I had never experienced anything like it.

o o o o o o o o o o o o o o o o o o o o o o o o o o o o o o o o

I was overwhelmed with what I had seen and heard. I had an incredible void in my life, was emotionally empty and depleted.

I knew that party was a first step, a preview into a new life that could really be something special. Bobby my new friend had asked me to study the bible and had a room for rent. To be continued in the water ingredient section; full disclosure.

Will share more about this first step later in the sweeteners section.

Lemons   Health Issues

This tent is wearing out...

News flash you have Diabetes. Not the message you want to hear from your Doctor. My A1C was 11 the doctor told me any higher and it's off to the hospital Was on my way back from a trip for work on a 6-hour drive home. It seemed like every 20 minutes I needed to make a rest stop. This was very unusual and alarming. I was not feeling well. Being the not going to the Doctor tough guy changed. As soon as I could I made a Doctors appointment . I must admit I was scared. I did not know what was wrong only that there was something wrong. I was overweight and was eating poorly. When faced with this health issue things could have taken a turn for the worse loosing what good health I had left. Sorry I had taken my health for granted there was only one choice that I needed to make and that was to do everything the Doctor said.

It seems like it always takes a life changing event to get my attention to change. I do not know at times how I am so blind to the Lemons that are prevalent in my life.

I put the blame on having a case of ***"Testosterone Poisoning. "***

More health issues…..

Some years ago, we as a family moved to the country.

It was like the old sitcom show GREEN ACRES. I had remarried and sold the business of 20 years I had started when wife #1 left. Nearly 2 decades had passed and it was time to leave the big city; or so I thought. I was eaten up with a major midlife crisis desperately wanting to reinvent myself. It wasn't the buy a Corvette that you cannot afford kind of midlife crisis it was the need to get out of dodge. A feeling trapped kind of feeling.

After selling a business and 3 homes, we bought an old 2 story carriage barn on 10 ½ acres cash. I will tell you more about the country life and house later in these pages.

Circling back to why I make mention this 2-story carriage barn /home is because a health issue arose from falling down a steep staircase dislocating my hip.

I remember crying in so much pain after I landed at the bottom of the stairs.

I was caring a big box that blocked my vison of the stairs and stepped on one of our cats which threw me tumbling down the stairs.

I did not go to the Doctors. I later developed arthritis in the hip many years later. The Lemons continued piling up, I put off getting a hip replacement for over 10 years. I was in daily writhing excruciating pain and could not take it anymore; finally getting an artificial hip.

The Ingredients needed to make Lemonade -The right stuff

Water   Soothing, Life Sustaining, Thirst Quenching

Summary: Water = Soothing

Water is necessary for life. It is the first thing scientists look for in space when searching for intelligent life. It is difficult to make lemonade without water. Our lemonade water comes to us in the form of things that sooth. If we are eating a proper diet and exercise regularly, we feel better. This section talks about the positive choices we can make. Making permanent positive lifestyle changes for life. This in turn helps us physically and mentally feel well. Fade diets and inconsistence with exercise will discourage you. Produce small incremental changes that add up to a big progress. Kaizen in Japanese means "good change" The culture of Japanese manufacturing, chooses small achievable goals, and executes. Lifestyles that include physical and mental wellbeing are like a fulcrum that help us power through obstacles, lifting heavy barriers.

With out water there is no life or lemonade.

In this case we are making references to an essential main ingredient to make figurative Lemonade using some creative license. Water is the bulk ingredient with no substitute. For our purposes the water references are things that soothe, sustain and quench our thirsty souls. As in real water there are many trace elements that are not visible to the naked eye. This is also true of the water in our figurative lemonade.

This reference to water will be about the things that are necessary for our quality of life like clean drinkable water. The information listed below will Help us to deal with the negative effects of the lemons on our bodies, minds and soul

Water-Soothing, life sustaining, energy giving

Our diet and its effects on our outlook.

Diet is something we can control. Our diets have effect on how we feel and look

I am talking about fuel for the body. Whether you are a formula 1 race car a 4-door sedan or a Mack truck you need the proper fuel. Hopefully you are not a Junker, if that's the case lets talk about a restoration. What changes can we make that will lead us to best performance. After overeating for so many years I found it hard to reign myself in. Primarily due to health concerns I needed to get serious about my diet. With diet and exercise as a lifestyle change, I slowly lost weight. I feel so much better now 25 pounds lighter. My cloths fit better, and I feel better about myself.

One thing that has been helpful to weight loss has been sharing my goal with someone that can keep me be accountable and provide encouragement as I work towards my goal weight.

I am not talking about going on a fad diet. To improve the lemonade we make, there needs to be wholesale changes that become a lifestyle. Let's say regular trips to **Golden Corral** *{an all you can eat restaurant}* should be avoided. This style restaurant should be for local livestock only. Off limits until we get our house in order. Way too much temptation there. The days of the AUCE chocolate fountain are over. We know that good choices can be made at the AYCE style buffets. The question is do you have the discipline?

Try not to skip meals it makes it harder for your body to assimilate your fuel. Eat often enough to maintain level blood sugar keeping your body regulated, steady.

The foods to avoid, main culprits are refined sugars, the evil carbs.

White Rice, Breads, Sodas these items cause spikes in your sugar levels. Alcohol is also an item to be avoided as it affects your sugar levels and is a depressant effecting your mood.

On the other hand, proteins help regulate and level the carbohydrates.

Eggs, Poultry, Sea Food, Tofu, Low Fat Greek Yogurt. I am not a nutritional expert but have learned a lot being diabetic. The reason I mention diet is that it controls how we feel. Affects our attitudes and moods. Having a Lifestyle that incorporate diet and exercise helps balance the flavor of the lemonade.

Fiber as part of our diets is also a great way to help control how we are feeling. Also known as roughage ,is the part of plant based foods

Oats, Beans, Pears, Peas, Brussel Sprouts are great sources of fiber and help boost your mood keeping you level. It passes thru the digestive system keeping it clean and healthy, easing bowel movements and harmful carcinogens out of the body. Fiber also helps us feel fuller longer. It can improve cholesterol and blood sugar levels assisting in preventing some diseases such as diabetes, heart disease and bowel cancer. Combining a balanced diet with exercise is very important.

Water-Soothing, life sustaining, energy giving

Exercise   Physical Activity

What type of physical activity do you enjoy? I firmly believe you will do something on a regular basis that you enjoy doing. Bike Riding, Rowing, Walking, all the ing's things. This does not include eating or talking, as physical exercise sorry. Moving your jaw is not exercise. I like walking, especially early morning watching the sunrise. Okay maybe this does not appeal to you. What physical activity can you do for 30 to 45 minutes 5 days a week? Start out small with 20 minutes a day and build up from there. Do something to get your body moving, burning calories. <u>Exercise combined with good diet is a game changer</u>.

This has been a key to help me deal with the lemons in my life. I seem to manage difficult situation when I have prepared for the day. I have a regular routine. I wake at 5am 5 days a week Get my exercise in and have time for some quiet reflection before work. This puts me in the right mindset before I start my day before most people are awake. Right about now you are saying no way this is not for me, that's fine. Make this lifestyle change work for you. I get it, I am one of those wake-up happy morning people you do not like. If you're the stay up late person that's great. Work your schedule out so you can be consistent. Consistency and frequency are very important.

How do you do this on vacation?

Let's say you're on a cruise find the deck where everyone walks and do your 45 minutes when it suits you. An activity like walking can be done everywhere. I came back from a 7-day cruise losing 2 pounds, eating well not starving myself. I dine on cruises using moderation combined with regular exercise.

Another example:

European trip I chose to backpack. The backpack held 2 weeks clothing.

Weighed about 17 pounds. Eating like a horse and lost 4 pounds. I walked everywhere and used public transportation. My point here is that I did not have a regular exercise time but was walking everywhere carrying a backpack that weighed 17 pounds. If you plan and make provisions for changes in your schedule you can still win. I like to use the word win when talking about these kinds of unusual circumstances because coming out ahead in diverse situations is winning. Winning breeds more winning; no one ever goes into a game wanting to lose. Winning and triumphing over the lemons makes more winning.

The Ingredients needed to make Lemonade -The right stuff

Water   Necessary for life

It is my opinion that a grounded spiritual life is necessary to squeeze the most difficult lemons in life. I am talking about the rip your guts out kind of lemons that can destroy you. The kind of lemons that kill you from the inside, hardening you. Joy robing making you cynical, old before your time.

You may be an atheist and have some way to reason why thing are the way they are. You may believe in GOD but do not have a real relationship with him grounded in his word.

As a friend I would like to tell you there is much more to living than just eating, sleeping and breathing. All of these are necessities for life but are you living? We can get to the point where we are just sick and tired of being sick and tired? Wrung out, feeling depleted. *Please give what I am about to share with you a chance.* I am not a bible scholar by any stretch. I would like to share my life's experience. Offering YOU an opportunity to triumph over this challenging complicated life we are living.

When I started studying the Bible with Bobby my life was being transformed from the inside out. The more I learned about GODS love for me the more at peace I was with myself. I learned what it meant to die to self and give the enormity of issues over to GOD. I shared with you earlier about my wife of 10 years leaving me for someone she met at work. The things that I read in GODS word has shown me how I needed to change. It revealed to me how selfish I am. It was very freeing knowing GOD could help me to change. I was not in this life's battle alone. I learned that I needed to take responsibility for the things that were wrong in my marriage and receive forgiveness from a loving GOD. He loves unconditionally and is fully aware how flawed I am. I learned about JESUS and how he loves. I saw him helping other flawed broken people like me.

One of my favorite stories about JESUS is when he meets a woman at a well. She came to the well to get water but left the well wanting to tell everyone about living water. The living water that wells up inside us. Gods spirit inside us changes everything. JESUS did not hold back with the woman he told her he knew how imperfect she was, and he still loved her offering her a new life. A way to deal with the lemons in her life. Forgiving her offering a new start. As I read more Bible and met GODS people it confirms my fundamental believe that GODS word is living and active relevant for life today. Amazing GOD could forgive when I could not forgive myself. I had made so many mistakes. Truly until I started learning about GOD it was all about me and me siting on the thrown of my life as king.

I worshipped my wife and material things as you would statues made of stone. I have learned we should not put our faith in flawed people but rather have faith in something perfect like JESUS. What a great example. JESUS related to all kinds of people in all kinds of circumstances. Showing what a life looks like when it is wanting to please GOD instead of man and mans traditions. This helped me deal with the mistrust I felt from the unfaithfulness and betrayal in my first marriage. Until I started studying the BIBLE, I did not know how out of whack my faith and core beliefs were. This awareness helped me Heal and learn to trust again. I knew the LORD would never disappoint me or walk out on me.

Water   Thirst Quenching

The continual lust for more. A thirst that would not be quenched. This was one of those BIG things GOD helped me with and continues to help with. True contentment and peace from a nagging inner voice. I had to learn that who I was as a person was not defined by what car I drove. The house I owned or the clothes I wore. I learned by having most of those things removed from me. What was also a valuable lesson was that happiness does not need to be postponed; I could be very happy with little in the present. We see this in people from countries that have little. Where does their joy come from?

Contentment and the mana principle. The Israelites after leaving Egypt's captivity needed nourishment, GOD provided everything the Israelites needed. The mana rained down from the sky. They were told, collect what you need for that day. This newly freed nation learned dependence/obedience on the Lord. Those who disobeyed found that the mana spoil. We must understand that if we are children of the living GOD, we are his child. What children are not taken care of by a loving Father? Maybe you did not have a loving earthly father. Perhaps you did not know your earthly father. I can honestly say the lord is a father to the fatherless. faithful in his care for his family. I am so grateful for everything big and small. Even when I was at my lowest low the lord always provided. I do not prescribe to the prosperity doctrine. The focus here is the generosity of the lord as a loving father. We see how faithful and generous the lord is when we are obedient to him as lord.

Stewardship is the belief that everything comes from GOD also belonging to him. I have a responsibility to care for the things I have been entrusted with. This takes such a burden off us when it comes to giving, either time or money. Understanding we need to be responsible with what we have been entrusted with.

Water   Cleansing

Romans 6:4   English Standard Version

We were buried therefore with Christ by baptism into death, in order that, just as Christ was raised from the dead by the glory of the Father we too might walk in newness of life.

Water cleansing water. The waters of baptism are an amazing thing.

There is nothing in the water that is magic. It is an amazingly supernatural opportunity for transformation, NEW BIRTH. At that time, you meet with the purifying blood of the Christ that changes everything. We will discuss this latter in the book under the sweeteners section.

Water Sleep-Rest

Sleep is important for 2 main reasons: It helps us repair and restore our organ systems including our muscles, immune system and various other hormones. It plays a crucial role in memory, helping us retain what we learn.

We cannot go without sleep. Without the proper amount of sleep there is a decrease in mental functions. The lack of sleep impairs the decision making prosses. Honestly when I do not sleep well, I am irritable a real grouch. The same goes for working 60 to 80-hour weeks.

There is a reason for a sabbath. We need time to reflect and repair. We are not machines. Working day after day with no breaks will make you unproductive. This also makes us prone to making mistakes that upset us. The frustration from the lack of rest will decrease our patience needed to push thru obstacles that while rested could have been done much easier. Beyond minor frustrations are fatal mistakes. Falling asleep while driving. Hopefully you are not working in an area like medicine that demands you not to make errors in judgment killing someone needlessly. It always scared me to hear the hours MD interns are required to work. Let's take stock of the amount of sleep, rest we are now getting and make the necessary changes that will help us deal with the lemons that come at us.

WATER Room to Breath

It is great to get away and unplug.

Go on a hiking or biking trip. Do anything out in nature to refresh yourself. Everyone is wired differently. The question is what works for you. Something I enjoy may frighten you to death. Or just the opposite I am not jumping out of a perfectly good airplane. Whatever the case plan a trip or event that will help you disconnect from the hectic pace of life. This intentional time spent, will pay large dividends giving you extra strength and energy toward making some exceptional lemonade.

Sweeteners   Life Enhancing and more

Summary: Sweeteners=Life Enhancing

Our sweeteners should be uplifting. The sweeteners help us to deal with the acidity from the lemons. Without sweeteners Lemonade is not drinkable. Explore the possibilities that bring sweetness to life. Some may be obvious, others often overlooked most disregarded. Consideration your desire for permanent positive change. Explore how adding sweeteners can improve the quality of the lemonade you create.

Faith based belief in something greater the greatest sweetener

Continued from the **surprise lemon** in this ingredients section. The story picks up where I am facing one of the biggest nastiest lemon's life can throw at you, divorce. As you recall my wife at the 8-year mark had an affair, the classic office romance. I would come to find out later that once divorced she married her coworker who had 2 small girls. This is all I know.

I had no children with my first wife and therefore no ties. When we parted ways at the courthouse that was the last time, I saw her.

We were separated for 2 years which put me at the 10-year married mark. I am not sure why things dragged out so long racking up large attorney fees. All I remember was spending 2 years on an emotional roller-coaster that was punctuated by financial negotiations. While the 2 years of separation played out, I drew closer to GOD going thru a lot of brokenness and healing. Making and drinking lots of lemonade. Was finally growing up as a person. A late bloomer.

In life the hardest lemons seem to have taught me the most. I am so grateful to have gone thru these hard lessons with GOD and GODS people helping me along the way. <u>This is the best sweetener and the key to making amazingly great lemonade.</u>

I had received a lot of good advice. One piece of advice was to try to reconcile the marriage, looking at the nation of Israel. Looking at its relationship with its creator as a model. The unfaithfulness of the nation of Israel must hurt the heart of GOD so much. I knew the covenant of my marriage was destroyed.

As a disciple of JESUS, I am called to be an imitator and learner with a humble heart. I proposed reconciliation, explaining the spiritual changes in my life. She wanted no part of it. Her mind was made up. I think asking for reconciliation was SO difficult because of the emotions of betrayal and a broken trust. This goes way beyond not wanting the stigma of divorce. Another positive thing about wanting to reconcile was there is no doubt as to how that story should finish. I have peace with how that terrible thing ended. I am Truly sorry for how things ended and how it must have hurt the lord.

Sweeteners   Life Enhancing and more

Having a life coach is so helpful.

Currently families are spread out. In the past we could often get advice from family members we respected and trusted. It was nice to have someone to relate struggles and goals.

I have moved a lot and found it hard to maintained close relationships with family members. Wherever I have lived I've had a life coach. Certainly, with the digital age we can have remote life coaching or advice from family Via What's App. That's great, if it works for you. My preference is to meet with someone face to face.

Accountability is an amazing tool that helps keep the ship on course and the lemonade sweet. We are not very objective of ourselves. It is great to have someone you respect and appreciate help guide, coaching you. Please understand how this relationship work. I would recommend having a set day and time that you could meet you're your coach.

Sweeteners   Read books that will encourage you

My first Recommendation and all-time favorite is the Bible. You cannot ask for a more encouraging and inspiring book. GOD inspired from cover to cover. You will learn more about yourself as you apply what you learn from the text.

FACTS ABOUT THE BIBLE:

- Over 40 Authors

- 3 Languages Hebrew, Aramaic, Greek

- Over 1500 years of writing

- One common thread of GOD'S relationship to man holding it all together

- Approximately 400 prophecies regarding Jesus in the Old Testament

What does the bible say about itself?

2 Peter 1:20-21

Men wrote the Bible, but they were "carried by the Holly Spirit"

Another great book is: *The New Evidence That Demands A Verdict* by Josh McDowell

Those are my top 2 books, there are so many more. The list could go on for pages

Sweeteners   Have the hope that this too will pass

It's nice to know how to make lemonade when you are in the middle of life's storm's I have been thru a few hurricanes. How is hurricane preparation like going thru storms in our lives.

- Understand the strength of the storm

- Do not underestimate the strength of your storm

- You can prepare for a positive outcome

- Have a plan that involves your creator

- Stay in a safe place until the storm passes

- Understand that the storm will pass over-this is temporary

Sweeteners   Have the hope that this too will pass [continued]

One of the sadist things you will hear is about someone who committed suicide because of **X-Y-or Z.** There is a bad breakup, someone loses a job, bad grades. I often wonder what makes someone feel so hopeless as to take their own life. Were the situations so bad where they needed to terminate their own existence?

I do not want to sound unfeeling; I understand people struggle with depression. There is a desperation that exists in situation where people think there is no way out.

Perhaps you are feeling this way, please talk to someone today. Counseling is not a shameful thing. We all need to talk to someone at different times in our life. Maybe your situation is not as bad as it seems. I have been in situations that have been resolved quickly and I have been in others that took 18 years to resolve. Patience is the key word here. Survey the situation. Get a grasp of the scope and depth of the severity of the problem.

Develop a plan of action. I often ask myself is doing nothing a plan. If this is your plan; how long are you going to do nothing? I have found ignoring a problem, the problems usual gets worse. Say its someone with operable cancer how would ignoring the problem help? In this case it would not because the cancer could spread and metastasize somewhere else. Everything has a custom solution. The challenge is to find the right solution that will help resolve the issue the best way. Take the example of my first marriage. I discover the infidelity. Next step-confront or ignore. I chose to confront-a separation and split up occurs-try reconciliation-that failed. Many things could have happened.

What could have happened?

- We could have reconciled got counseling - worked things out

- Could have gone on a rage and hurt or killed both Wife and Lover.

- Gone to prison for the rest of my life

- Committed suicide

You see how this could have played out. The best choice- was to have patients and work on improving myself. Started learning how to make lemonade by coming to faith putting my trust in GOD and GODS people. Gleaned wisdom and encouragement from GODS word and GODS people.

The 2 years in limbo could have been 5 years, I was prepared to do what ever it took to see the broken relationship either mended or ended. Turns out it ended. Ending in the best possible way it could. There were irreconcilable differences on her part. She wanted to go her own way. I wanted to do it GODS way. We see how when we react in a sensible way, not overreacting things will go well for us.

Acting on emotion would have taken me down a slippery slope of disaster. What if I chose badly and committed suicide? I would have missed out on sharing my life with you. Not known what an awesome marriage could be like doing things GODS way. Get a second chance to do things right. Experiencing a honeymoon night that was really my honeymoon night. This time having a pure dating relationship.

Surly I had baggage to sort out. This time I married a GODLY woman who is kind and patient with me. There is so much great stuff I would have missed if I did not take up the art of lemonade making.

SWEETNERS   Throw out the negative tapes that keep playing in your mind

I have a hard time clearing out my clothes closet

My closet is a mess. I need to go thru and donate cloths that do not fit any more.

I am not sure why I struggle with this so much. Perhaps I am not ready to part with these items. Maybe one day I could wear this or that. I am sure this is due to sentimentality. I think, it would be nice to have the extra room in my closet. Uncluttered. It is dangerous to compare my overstuffed closet to my mind. Oh well here I go. There are times my mind is so cluttered with old useless thoughts that do not fit. Why run old movies that have no benefit to the present; here comes that word again. *Sentimentality-Noun* excessive tenderness, sadness, or nostalgia.

This definition covers it. Some of this is good most of it is bad even harmful. Sometimes your mind is flooded with filler that needs to be donated like my old clothes that do not fit anymore. How can I empty my head of old junk taking up valuable space? My positive nature is often at war with the past and its failures. Why run those tapes anymore especially things I have been forgiven of? Costly debts that were paid for in full by way of JESUS on the cross.

Sweeteners   The attitude of gratitude

Take stock is some of the smallest things today. Time is not guaranteed to anyone, Tempest Fugit Latin "Time Flies". Make a list, you will be amazed how much you should be grateful for. What people are you grateful for? The friends you have. Shelter, air conditioning, a bed to sleep in it sounds simple. It is easy to take for granted things that a lot of people do not have Thankful I can walk, talk, eat.

Use the bathroom myself. Have shoes. Writing these things down makes you grateful because we do not think about not having those things or abilities. we do not appreciate things until it's too late. These things when lost and not appreciated may never be regained. That's especially true about people. I think of the things I wish I had said or done for someone that no longer are taking breaths on this earth.

You never know when someone's time on this earth is over. Tell people how you love them. Mend a fence with that Sister or Brother, Uncle, Cousin, Friend etcetera.

Try this, hand write a thank you card to someone for something when you are feeling sad and ungrateful. you will be amazed how that can change the way you look at things and lifts your spirits. Not to say what it will do for someone receiving the handwritten card a rare thing in this age of its all about me.

Sweeteners Giving, serving others

Winston Churchill said- ***"We make a living by what we get.***
We make a life by what we give."

True words,

Love this quote especially the last part*;" **We make a life by what we give."***

I am convinced givers are the happiest people on the planet!

It is so fulfilling to serve people. We are wired to be givers unfortuity not everyone is aware of that. I wasn't. I did not figure this one out until later in life.

Once I got started, I can't stop. It is an incredible feeling to know you made a difference in someone's life. I know I am not the only one that has experienced this. I was reading a story about a man who in 2001 was waiting for his truck to be fixed at a Ford dealer in Newport News VA. While he was waiting, he read an article in National Geographic about a bridge that needed to be repaired in Ethiopia. The picture in the magazine showed 10 men on broken bridge holding a rope while the person crossing the broken span shimmied across a rope that spanned the broken-out area of the bridge. One slip and they would fall to their death. The name of the bridge was Sebara Dildiy.

In the highland's language of Ethiopia, the name translated to Broken Bridge.

The man at the Ford dealership was so moved; he gathered some people and supplies and went to repair the bridge. He said, "broken bridges equal broken lives". This Sixty-year-old building contractor knows what it is to help people. Without the bridge the next passable span to cross the Blue Nile river was a 1 week walk up stream.

By 2006 he built 50 bridges traveling to Asia, Africa, South America building suspension foot bridges and changing lives. The man's name is Ken Frantz; he started a Not for Profit called Bridges to Prosperity. The 50th bridge was a rebuilding of the first bridge in Ethiopia that was broken again during floods.

There have been a lot of partners added to the bridge building efforts. A Swiss firm Helvetias has helped train and organize efforts on a large scale. Involvement by private and public companies has been strong. Everyone that hears about the projects wanted to contribute.

This Includes Shipping Ports who have donated recycled cables and ropes, contributing material for free. These materials are loaded into shipping containers and sent to destinations where they are needed.

If the local peoples are willing to help, Bridges to Prosperity will get the materials to the site. The not for profit also trained locals and volunteer's how to construct the bridges. Since the first bridge build in 2001. Bridges to Prosperity has built over 245 bridges helping more than 920,000 people in 20 countries with the help of volunteers from the Rotary Clubs and industry. The people that have served and contributed have had a direct impact on diminishing rural isolation. These efforts have improved the lives of countless remote peoples.

There are so many needs, it is not hard to find people in your own city that need help. Be like Ken to get things going. Start a serving revolution, change the world. One man reading the National Geographic's at a Ford dealer improved a lot of lives for a decade. Improving people's lives living in poverty who needed it the most.

○ ○

Sweetener Forgive and forget

Forgiveness is a very potent sweetener. A little goes a long way, a lot goes even further. Forgiveness and humility mix well and complement each other. This is true with both giving and receiving forgiveness. There are people that do not know how to say, "I am sorry". These Folks are never wrong. Ask them they will tell you. To them, everyone else is wrong. These are the always right people that populate the earth. What would a planet be like if they were in charge? Can you imagine the chaos? The tension? A true dictatorship of rightness all the time.

The hatred? Everyone would be nuking each other. Now on the other hand imagine a planet where all the people apologized and extended forgiveness to one another what a beautiful place it would be. Sounds like heaven. Forgiveness frees the soul, gratitude and love heal it. It takes a stronger person to forgive. The weak do not forgive easily and continue in their weakness building a prison of regret. The only key for freedom of the soul is forgiveness. Are you a prisoner? Can you forgive others, or yourself?

When you get wounded, the hurt is one of the hardest things to deal with especially if the hurt is fresh. The cuts need to heal. Maybe this is as a gash that is so deep it needs professional help. Here is a test: If the bleeding does not stop you need professional help. If it is a long period of time and you are still hurting, get help.

It's not like in the war movies where the hero is wounded. He or she opens a bullet putting the gun powder on the open wound; ignites the gun powder, there's a flash. Magically the wound seals up, that's Hollywood. Works in the movies you say, we are in the real world. The idea of time healing wounds is truer to life.

Counselling is not a bad option. Perhaps talking to a trained professional is what is needed. Forgiveness mixes well with our figurative life sustain water. Forgiveness is a necessary sweetener an ingredient that cannot be substituted. Just think how nice that glass of lemonade is going to taste as your wounds heal. Drink up, squeeze more lemons make some more lemonade pour another glass.

And repeat……. Drink up, squeeze more lemons make some more lemonade pour another glass.

Variations of the recipe

Attitude Is Everything

There are various circumstances in which our figurative lemonade may taste and look different.

It is where you make and drink your lemonade that makes a difference. Packaging and storage have been known to cause variations effecting taste. Glasses may make us think it tastes different but that's only in our heads- frosted glass, mason jar, shot glass its all the same. Going down the same way.

Attitude Is Everything in the workplace

Keep it professional:

Charles Swindoll said *"I am convinced that life is 10% what happens to me and 90% of how I react to it. So, it is with you…. We oversee our attitudes"*

The workplace is the true testing grounds for our attitudes and how we communicate both verbally and non-verbally.

Do not discount body language, body language can speak louder than our words. Professor Albert Mehrabian of University of California in Los Angeles combined the statistical results of two studies and the results were Non-verbal communication that is made up of body language is 55% and tone of voice 38%. Okay your way ahead of me where is the 7% that is missing. I think that he is trying to make a point. Previously the rule of thumb was 7 % verbal 93 % non-verbal. I found this information on the internet it must be true….

Another tidbit I got from the internet is success is 10% inspiration and 90% perspiration, this one makes me want to check my deodorant to see if it is still working. Hold on let's do our own math here. If my attitude is right working hard at it 90% of the time my 55% non-verbal skills will carry me the rest of the way helping me succeed. Sorry, is my thinking flawed? What do you think?

Nothing wrong with having fun with numbers the IRS has been doing that for years. Speaking of numbers how about that performance appraisal. Do all the numbers line up on the exceeds expectations section?

If so, keep on doing what you have been doing. If not, perhaps your attitude needs an adjustment. Attitude can cost you and lighten up your wallet where you feel it. Granted we are all flawed no one has the best attitude all the time. All we can do is win more than we lose. No one likes to lose especially at work.

Attitude Is Everything at home

Home is where the heart is and should be. Our home should be a place of refuge not refuse. I was told that I said NO a lot. I started thinking about that. Why was I not more accommodating? More helpful around the house. I must take this into greater consideration.

Perhaps you are a care giver what consideration has been extended to you?

Care givers are in an especially difficult position and do not have the luxury of saying no. I think I needed to become more of a leader servant. This model is good for people leading households, Businesses, Churches. leading with love is very effective. Once we realize that our tool kit contains more than a hammer, everyone benefits. What is the tone we set at home? How are we fostering positive culture at home? If you are living alone, how do you treat yourself. I do not say this to be funny. I really mean, how do you make your home a happy place to be. Do you like having guests? Do you initiate with others show hospitality? The last thing you want is to have your home be a place where you hide from the world putting barriers and concertina wire around windows and doors. Do you feel lonely? Why not you be the person to organize something in your home. You say you have limited resources, have a potluck dinner, lunch. You may think up all kinds of excesses, not to have people into your home. The place needs painting. I need new furniture. I will have to clean the house. The place is too small. I will leave some space and you can put your custom excuse in the blank_____....

Okay, thanks for indulging me I was running out of excuses how about you....

Boy, I can be so annoying sometimes, sorry.

Attitude Is Everything when you're out and about

How do you treat people in the service industry? Are you a generous person? Not only TIPS but with your attitude towards people? What cost you more a thank you or 15% TIP. How about doing both, which is appreciated more?

To Improve Promptitude this is an invention from England 17 th century. While traveling thru Europe I learned that leaving a TIP is not always the best thing to do. Some Europeans can be offended because they feel they are already being paid to serve you. Customs and culture very but it is never a bad thing to show earnest appreciation for a job well done!

Saying "Thank You" cost you nothing; perhaps it means more to someone having a tough day to hear some words of encouragement. Some sweeteners for the lemons they are processing to make their lemonade that day. We do not understand the power we have at our disposal to improve the quality of someone else's life. Everyone is going thru something. Be liberal with the figurative sweeteners.

I will let you in on a secret.

As you are giving away sweetener the quality of your lemonade improves exponentially. You will find yourself becoming a lemon processing expert.

When out and about driving; does your positive attitude shine like a polished hood ornament. We all struggle with patience sitting in traffic. Lots of things can happen while you are in a car including road rage. The lemons in this category can seriously kill or cripple if not managed well.

Please Please Please. If you find yourself angry behind the wheel count to ten- or fifty if you must. Do not overreact. That vehicle is a weapon with someone angry behind the wheel. Vehicular homicide is serious, once in prison you will have a whole other set of lemons to process. You could be drinking lemonade by the gallons waring an orange jump suit. Losing your freedom is very sad in so many ways. So much strife can be avoided if you can cool down. People also keep guns in cars which is another good reason not to aggravate or harass your fellow drivers. You do not want to die of lead poisoning!

Attitude Is Everything while traveling.

Traveling is one of my favorite things to do. Understandably traveling can also be stressful if you do not know the language or have GPS.

Using public transportation is often stressful. Big City planers understand how getting yourself around a large city is difficult. I have some tips for you that may alleviate some stress.

These are lemon squeezers.

- Put the city's transit app on your phone this will help you know the transit lines and times of departure and arrival. Some city's apps have live GPS tracking you can watch public transit in real time.

- Purchase a bulk fare card as opposed to individual per ride fare cards. For example, 24-hour pass. If you have a smart phone with you can purchase your tickets online, using your phone as the ticket.

- An extreme example is all in one card, in Lisbon Portugal, using the Lisboa Card you can access most public transportation, Museum's and other popular sites as well. Great value very convenient. There were very few things that needed to be payed separately like the ferry.

- If you are in a hurry and need to get to the Airport get an UBER well worth the money.

- If you have a long layover and are leaving the airport to sightsee pay to store your bags in Philadelphia Pa, for instance I payed $10 a bag for 6 hours of rental.

Attitude Is Everything when spending time with family

If your family is like mine, you are spread out over the continent and perhaps another continent. When planning family reunions tough decisions on location come into play. True its hard to all agree but we all try to be flexible and try to meet once a year. Once you all make it to the destination, compromise is the best sweetener. There is the where are we going to eat, do and see that always needs to be worked out. You do not see each other very often make it as pleasant as posable. You do not need to push buttons that you know bring up sad unfortunate things from the past. Enjoy each other's company isn't that why you wanted to get together to start with? Keep it light enjoy being patient and considerate, love one another.

Attitude Is Everything when things get gritty

"Life happens" is a saying that's familiar to us. Grit is an irritant and is abrasive. Situations and people can fall into this category. This is a broad subject that covers a lot of ground. Both situations with people and abrasive situations cannot often be avoided. If you know prior to entering a situation can you do some attitude preplanning? Aim high to hit your target. Then at least you do not feel as though you were ambushed or worse mugged. Sorry this section fell out after the family section. I must say though It is family that can be the grittiest, abrasive at times. The saddest thing is when families are not talking to each other for this reason for that reason. It usually is something petty and mundane. As with everything else love conquers all. You be the peace maker forgive and mend that fence. Regrets are a terrible thing. While that person is still alive try to work things out. Why should others in your family suffer because you had an unresolved disagreement. Be the bigger person and make a pitcher of lemonade to share. The world is fractured enough why be alienated from the one you should be closest to. Enough said just do it.

Dealing with Past

Leaving the past in the past

Seeds-Stopping seeds from taking root

Lemon seeds from the figurative variety of lemons are very toxic. These seeds if not disposed of properly will take root in your heart and destroy any joy you may have, choking you making everything you touch and see sour. Please avoid handling these seeds. The seeds have powers to pull you back into the past. These seeds are full of hate, anger and frustration. Look at the seeds as hazardous waste. Handle with care; destroy seeds while juicing.

Dealing with Past - Leaving the past in the past

Peels-Useful protection shielding the past

It is hard to believe that a figurative lemons peel is useful in repelling the past. The skin is fragrant, smelling fresh. The oils in the skin help the past just slide off. Allowing the past to stay in the past. The peel is the most useful and a positive part of such a sour destructive fruit. It is ironic that something so good covers something so bad. That proves that everything that looks good on the outside is not necessarily good on the inside. After deeper investigation the truth comes out, the juice also

Dealing with Past - Leaving the past in the past

Pulp-Some people like pulp Pulp is like the past, good to learn from. The pulp reminds us of the past but has little value in the present and therefor is no threat. Pulp is neutral it was used to hold the Figurative lemon juice and has served its purpose. Not sure why people like pulp....

Whether you are just learning the art of lemonade making or are an experienced producer; life has its way of providing great lessons to be learned. I hope you have gotten some tips from what was shared in these pages. There is also a workbook which is separate from this book. The workbook is designed to help you deal with issues, pulling them out of your head and heart. I also recommend journaling on some of the questions from the workbook as the few lines offered may not come close to getting to the root of what you are trying to express. Thanks for your interest in these pages as I willingly want to share my heart with you. Hardship is a task master and methodically needs to be dealt with.

Make some lemonade drink in the peace….

www.ingramcontent.com/pod-product-compliance
Lightning Source LLC
Chambersburg PA
CBHW020438030426
42337CB00014B/1306